TREASURE HUNTING TIPS

BY

Michael Mosley

I dedicate this book to all the folks in the world who seek for lost or hidden treasure. And the Good Lord above who watches over all.

This book is meant to be a source of information and inspiration to the reader. I hope that it inspires the reader to go out into the sunshine and search for whatever form of treasure he or she desires to find. If so, then good luck and God bless.

I have been involved in a fantastic hobby over the years. I started at the age of 20 with a used metal detector that had a broken discriminator on it. I found mostly junk with that machine, but it did allow me to start enjoying a hobby that was fascinating and possibly profitable. As I recall, I found a few clad coins at the beach with it, but nothing to write home about. I did learn that a metal detector with a broken discriminator was a big hassle to use. 2/3rds of the finds I made were trash items simply because that discriminator was broken. If the disc control would have been working properly, I would have been able to skip a lot of that junk and find more good items in my searches. That detector was a D handle type. Which meant that it had a handle sort of shaped like a letter D.

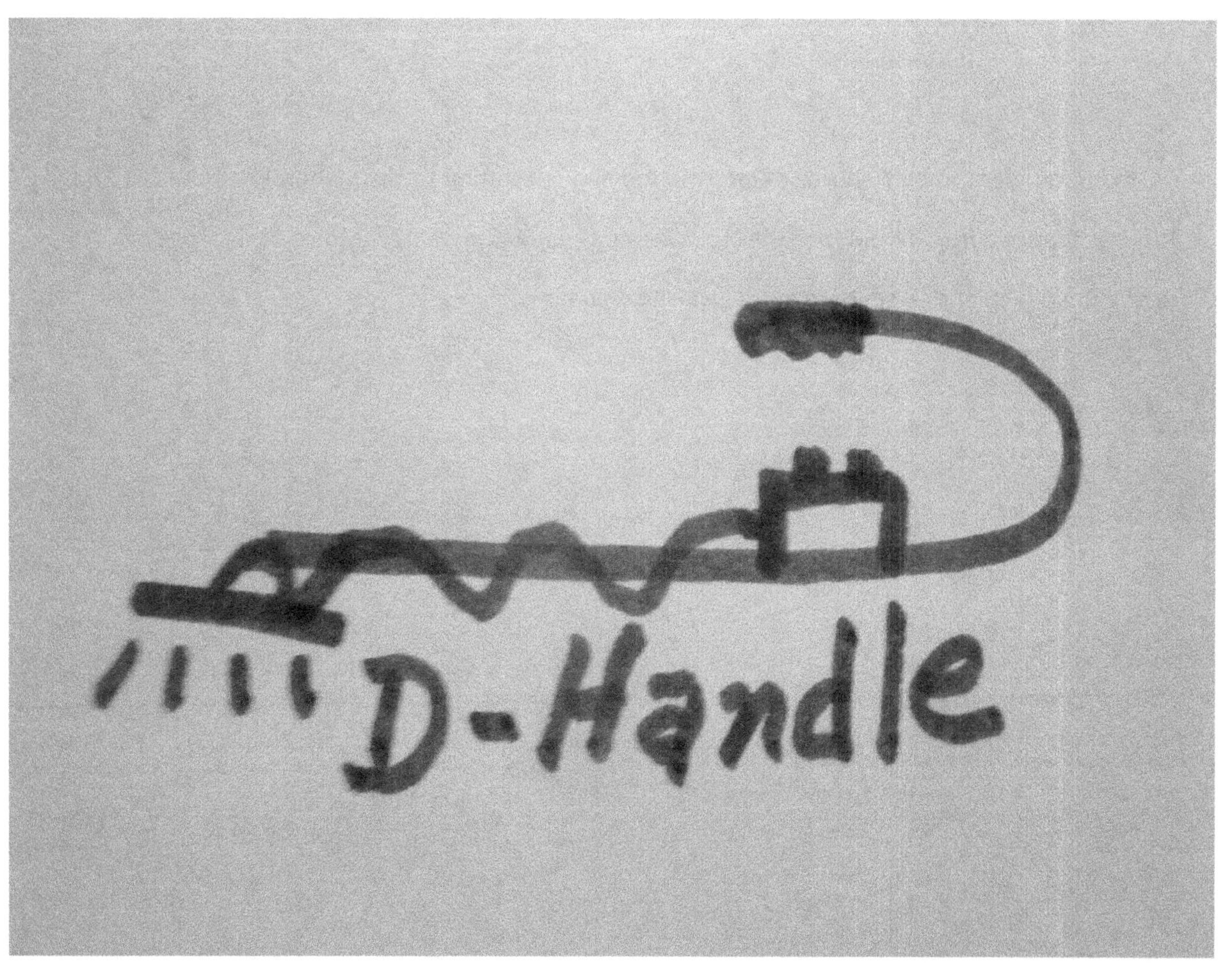

The D handle was a very popular type handle back in the 1970's. The detector that I bought with the broken discriminator on it was an older model TR detector. TR stood for Transmitter Receiver and was a standard operating system for metal detectors back in the early 1970's. One thing that was good about TR machines was that you could hold the coil still and it would still pick up a target. Most modern detector coils have to be swung over targets in order to pick up a signal. They are Motion Detectors—in order to get a signal at all, the search coil must be swung from side to side. After using the detector with the broken disc control a few months, I sold it at a pawn shop and cut my losses. But that urge to get out into the world to search for treasure had been started with a great pull. I eventually bought another detector that had a working disc setting on it and went to work trying to find some goodies. As I recall, that machine had a different type of handle on it.

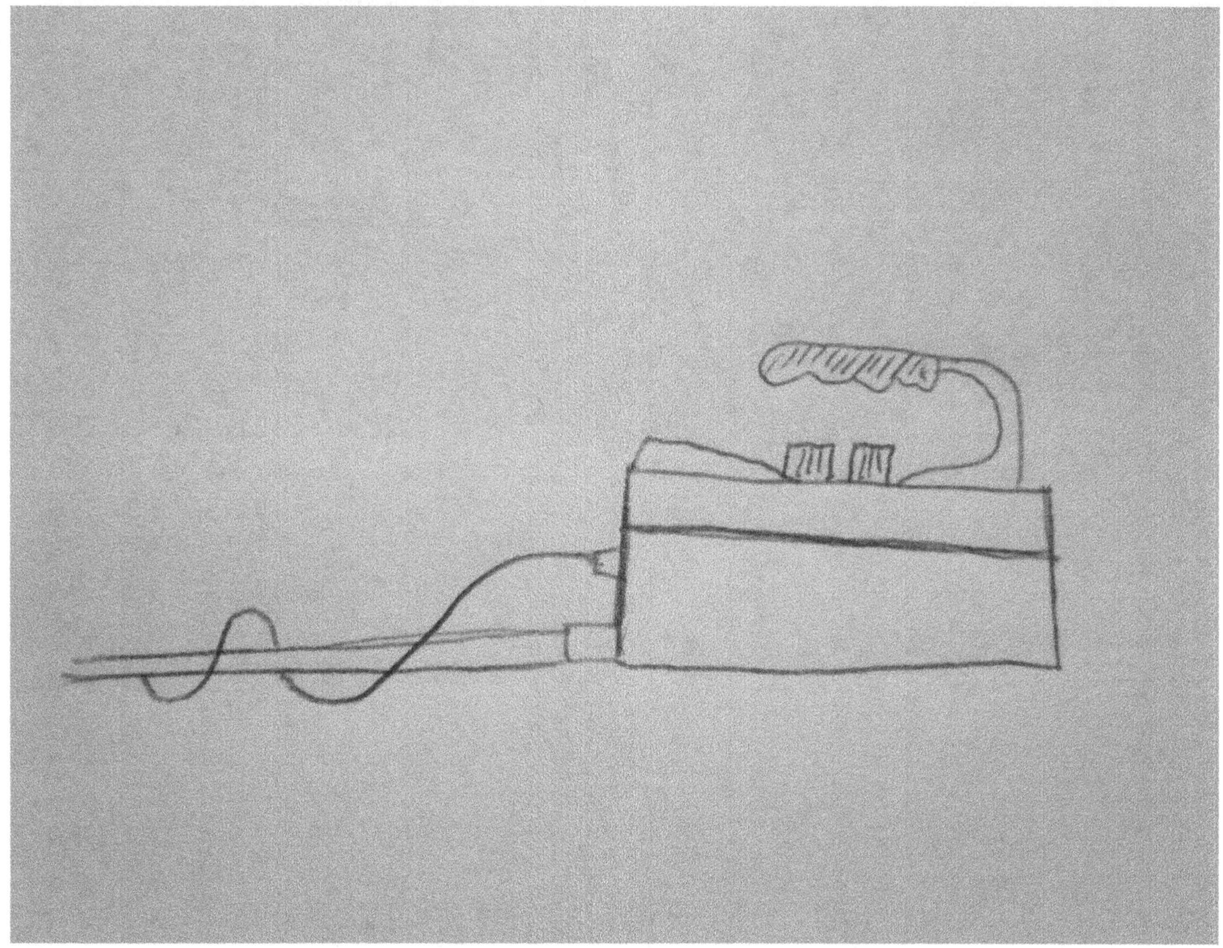

These handles were popular back in the 70's also and after using them for a few hours, a person's wrist would begin to ache. Some of us detectorists thought of them as wrist-breakers. So the industry decided to come up with a different style of handle that wouldn't be as wearing on people's wrists. The S handle was well accepted by detectorists because it is very comfortable to use. A person can hunt all day without much stress on the wrist or arm.

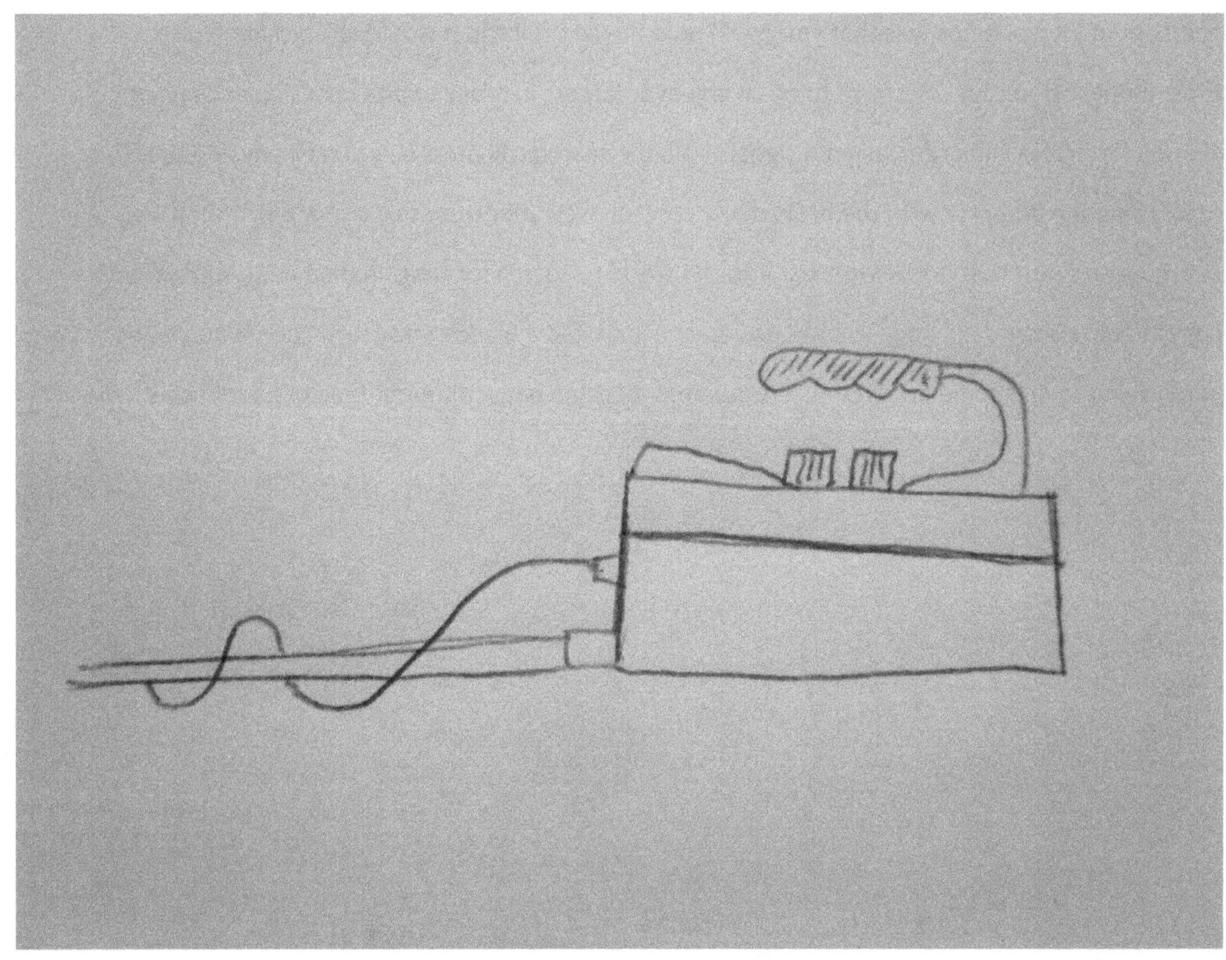

One picks up many tips along the way. No one can be an expert from the start. It takes time to become a seasoned and knowledgeable metal detectorist/treasure hunter. One of the first things to learn is that there are more junk targets in the ground than good targets. Items such as nails, wire, foil, pull-tabs, etc.

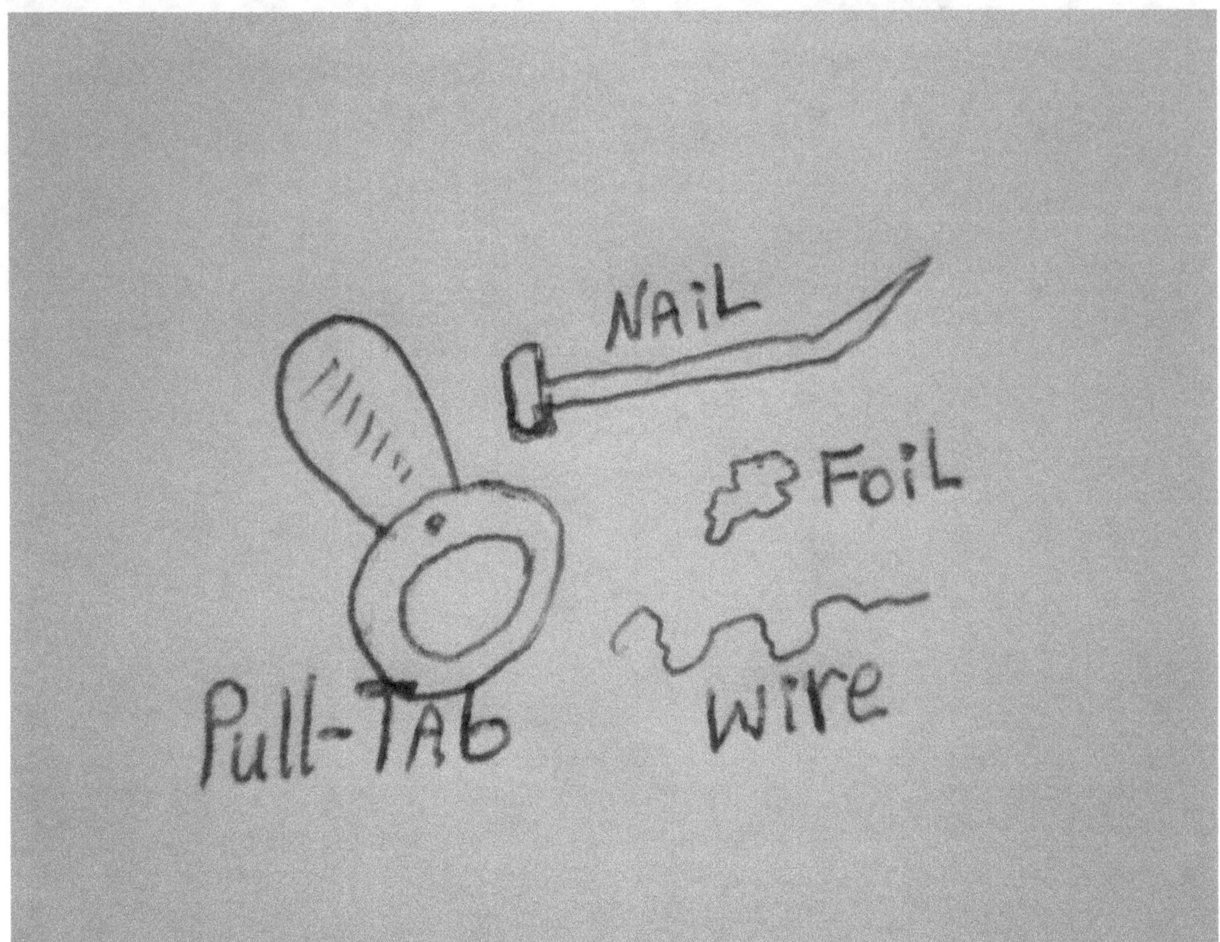

Rusty old nails, pieces of tin foil and wire, pull-tabs, bottle caps, and other junk are in almost every site that can be searched. In recreational parks, there usually will be plenty of pull-tabs and other junk in the ground left behind by the people who visit the park each day. I usually turn the disc level on my detector up to where it won't pick up pull-tabs and bits of wire and nails. I set the disc to below the nickel range so that the machine will only pick up coins and other items that read from a nickel or other US coin that is above the foil range on my machine. If I didn't do that, then I'd have to constantly dig up pull-tabs, foil, and other junk items that are of no use to me. Of course, by doing so, I will be eliminating the possibility of finding some smaller gold items such as small gold rings. But I will still be able to pick up some larger gold rings that fall into the nickel range of the detector.

There are elements in the ground that can cause interference to your detector. Sometimes a detector can begin to act very erratically. Especially when detecting underneath high voltage power lines. When this occurs, the only options are to leave that area or turn the sensitivity way down on your detector where you won't pick up the interference as much. Sometimes it may be impossible to stay in that area without some interference.

When detecting really close to metal objects such as playground equipment, it may be necessary to turn the sensitivity setting way down so that you can operate the detector near that metal object.

When searching on the beach, you may have to turn the sensitivity level on your detector way down to be able to operate the machine more effectively. Turning the sensitivity down may be the only option if you want to be able to find a few good items in the wet salt sand. Typically, wet salt sand causes problems for a VLF (Very Low Frequency) detector. Most metal detectors are of the VLF type nowadays. If you are going to be hunting a lot in wet salt sand, I'd suggest getting a PI (Pulse Induction) detector. PI machines don't have much trouble with the wet salt conditions of a beach. The only drawback, is that they don't discriminate out trash and you have to dig everything—even the junk targets. Another type machine that works well in salt conditions is a multi-frequency type detector. These have discrimination ability, but can be pretty costly machines. But they are worth the money when it comes to not having to dig up so much junk. I've used PI machines for water hunting and I have to dig junk over a foot deep all during the hunt. That can get old quickly. When water hunting, you need a long-handled beach scoop to recover the targets in the water. I recommend a stainless-steel scoop with 5/8th inch holes in it so that it will sift out the sand and debris faster. Smaller holed scoops can retain small items such as ear ring studs, but will take longer to sift out the sand and debris. I would go with the 5/8th inch hole version if I was you. 5/8TH inch holes won't allow a US dime to fall through and that's good enough for me.

Long-Handled Scoop

Sometimes when detecting a site, you may come across a coin that is standing on its side or edge. A detector can have more trouble finding a coin in such a position. Basically, detectors are surface readers and not mass readers. So, a coin lying on its side can't present much surface area for the search coil to read and give a signal. You have to listen for a faint signal to even have a chance to find a coin standing on its edge. To hear those faint signals, one needs a decent pair of headphones.

A decent pair of headphones will allow you to hear much better the signal coming from the detector. And when detecting at a beach with the waves crashing ashore and the sea gulls squawking and people Being loud, a pair of decent headphones will allow you to be able to hear signals much better. Most Headphones manufactured for detecting have volume control settings. And some headphones are equipped with sound magnifying ability so that a person can hear the faintest deepest target signals With no problem. Some of these types can be quite costly ($100-$200), but some folks swear by them and believe that their find rates are much higher because of them.

Some folks use a handkerchief to lay the excavated dirt on while they are recovering a coin or ring, etc. This way they can be sure to pour all the dirt back into the excavation when the coin or other item is recovered.

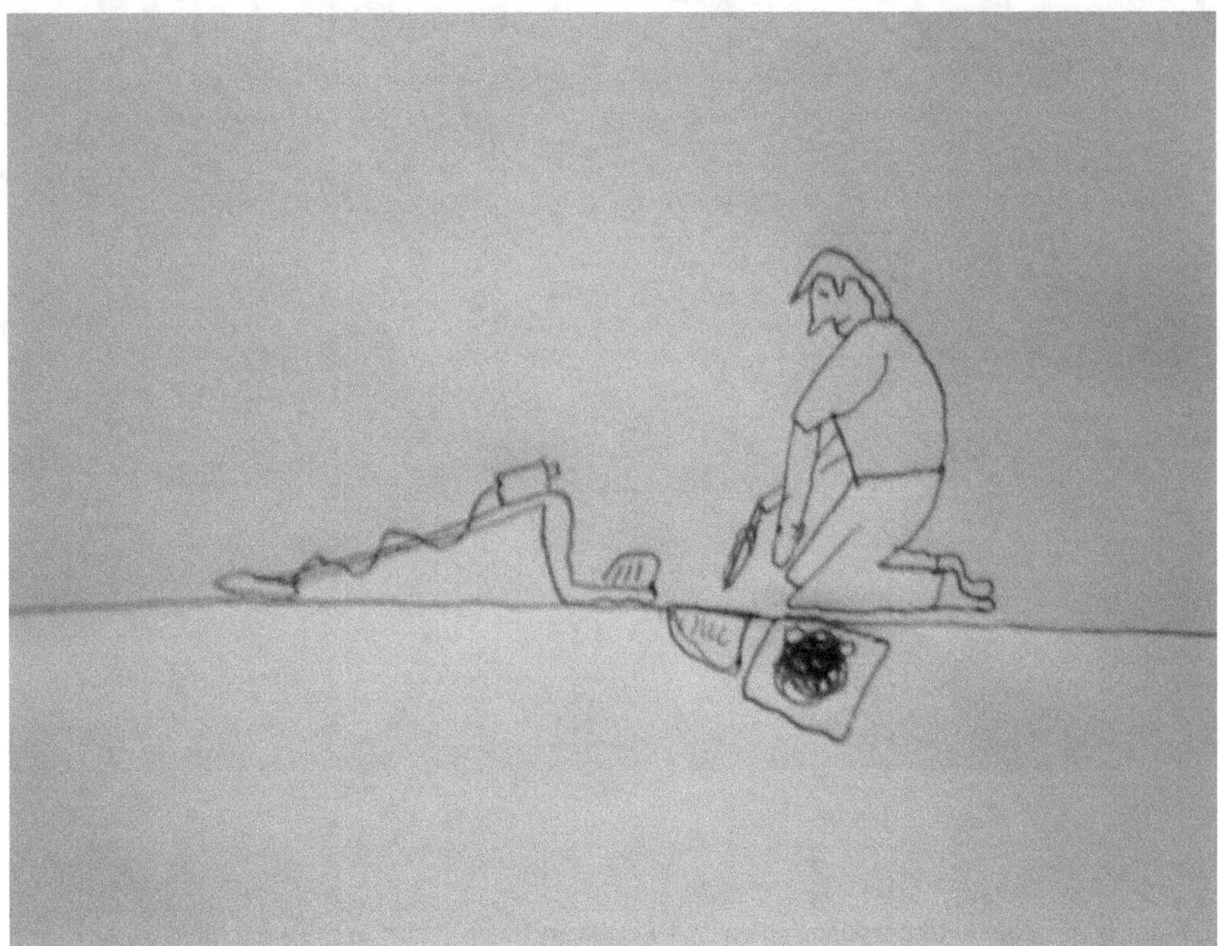

Some folks don't look too kindly at folks making a mess of their yard/lawn. As a matter of fact, most folks don't like someone who is making a mess while digging around in a yard. So the hanky idea is a good one. Another thing that folks use for the purpose of putting the excavated dirt on, is a Frizbee or whatever you call those throwing discs that folks like to throw down at the park or beach.

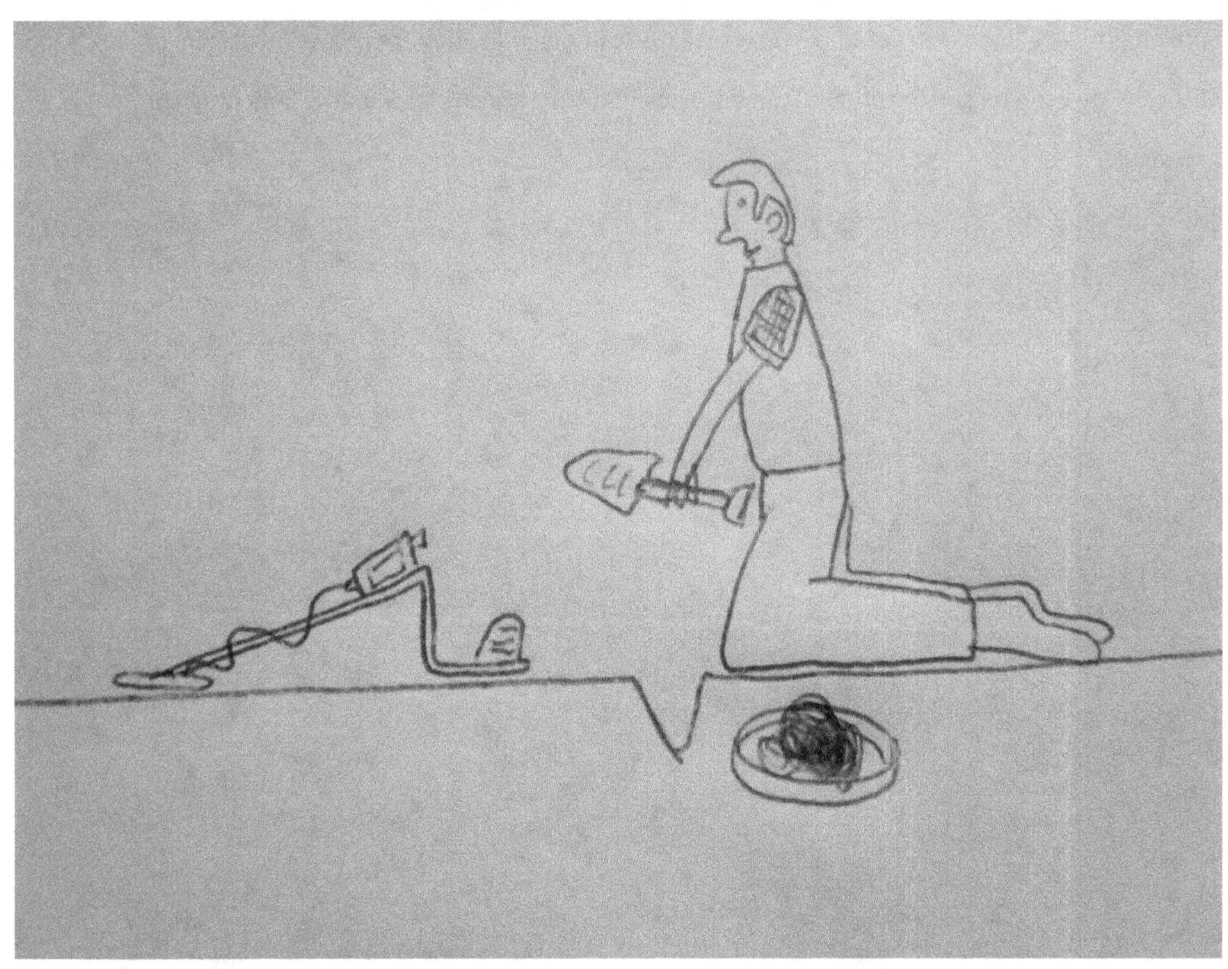

The disc is very easy to tote around and doesn't weigh very much at all. Put the dirt in the disc, and when you have recovered the target, pour the dirt back into the hole and place the grass back like it should be and tamp it down with your hand or your foot. Easy as it gets. Then pick up your detector, digging tool, and disc and go on searching until the next target. And repeat the process.

Metal detector meters come in all sorts of configurations. But, in general, they will have designations on them for different types of metal.

The ferrous metal such as iron will always read to the left side of a meter. The coins will begin at nickel level and go to the right side of the meter or as some folks refer to it as the higher side of the meter. If you set the disc setting at just before nickel level, then you will not be able to pick up small iron targets and tin foil, etc. Of course, larger pieces of iron may be picked up no matter how the detector is adjusted because it will over ride the detectors ability to disc it out. Finding iron isn't a bad thing when you are relic hunting. Many relics are made of iron and so finding them is a good thing. But in most cases, iron isn't what you are looking for. Most people hope to find coins and jewelry when they are detecting a site.

Cache Hunting : A cache is anything of value hidden or lost by someone in the past. Hunting for a cache isn't exactly the easiest way to fill your pockets up with valuables. People have been known to have searched for years and never found what they were looking for. But some folks get lucky and actually find a buried or hidden cache of coins or other valuables to justify all the effort they have put into searching. Some folks come up empty-handed, and some folks come up smelling like roses, as folks sometimes say. That's how the old ball bounces sometimes. You are lucky, or you are not. PERIOD! Cache hunters use larger-diameter search coils that can cover more ground quickly and get more depth. Most caches were probably not buried any deeper than one could reach down to. Sometimes people would put in a few more coins, or take a few out as needed. But most caches were buried and left alone for safe-keeping. Many have long since been forgotten or either the burier or hider has tried to go back and find it but had no luck locating it. Some cache owners never got back to their cache or caches because they died and couldn't get back to them. As I say, a large search coil is best for cache hunting because of the depth that they can get.

Searching for gold nuggets is something that brings some folks good luck. They search through mine tailings and down dry washes to find traces of gold. Some detectorists search the shallows of rivers and streams for gold and some get lucky. Manufacturers make detectors that are specialized for searching for gold. These detectors have a highly-boosted gain on them (Boosted sensitivity) and have frequencies that are more suited for finding gold. In general, a detector for finding gold will have a higher frequency than one made for normal detecting such as coin hunting or relic hunting. Higher frequencies are more able to find gold, and lower frequencies are more suited to cache hunting or relic hunting. Some folks find small gold flakes, and some find nice-sized nuggets.

Even small-sized nuggets can be sold to jewelers. Jewelers can make some nice jewelry out of gold nuggets. The larger the gold nugget, the more the gold nugget is worth. A gold nugget can be worth 3 or 4 times as much if it is a nice size and looks interesting.

Some places to search: AVOID FEDERALLY-PROTECTED AREAS SUCH AS STATE PARKS AND ANYWHERE ELSE WHERE METAL DETECTING AND TREASURE HUNTING IS PROHIBITED. CHECK THE LAWS CONCERNING THE AREA THAT YOU WANT TO DETECT AND ALWAYS HAVE PERMISSION—PREFERABLY IN WRITING BEFORE CONDUCTING A SEARCH.

Places you may be able to search:

1. Parks-beach parks, city parks, etc.
2. Playgrounds-at schools, and elsewhere.
3. Church yards.
4. Old home sites.
5. Hunting camp sites.
6. River landing sites.
7. Farm fields.
8. Ball fields.
9. Community center grounds.
10. Courthouse grounds.
11. Picnic areas.
12. Any place (Where it is legal to do so) where Civil War activity once happened.
13. Any place where Revolutionary War activity once happened that is legal to search.
14. Hillsides where kids used to slide down in snow or on straw.
15. Old horse racing tracks and grounds.
16. Fishing camps and fishing holes or swimming holes.
17. The grounds around hunting lodges or ski lodges.
18. The grounds underneath ski lifts.
19. Family reunion sites.
20. Wedding sites.

Some detectorists carry small flags with them to stick into the ground wherever a target

is heard, and after detecting for a while, they go back and uncover the targets wherever the

flags are stuck in the ground. They do this in soil or in beach sand.

Some folks may think that that would be a silly way to metal detect, but it really is just a matter

of choice. What one treasure hunter likes or dislikes may not be what another treasure hunter

likes or dislikes. "Whatever floats your boat." As the folks used to say.

A floating sifter is a good thing to use when detecting in calm water. Just dig up a target,

and throw the debris in the scoop into the floating sifter and the water will wash out the

sand and debris. Then you inspect the screen to see if there are any good items in the sifter.

Floating sifters are usually made with a wooden box made up of 1" x 4" lumber with a wire

or plastic screen attached to the bottom. I usually nail some thin wood strips to bottom to

hold the screen into place. Hardware cloth with ½" holes in it makes a good sifter screen for

a floating sifter.

Some people like to start a spiral-patterned search pattern whenever they make a find

on a beach. Some swear by this method and claim that it helps them recover far more

Good targets on a beach because objects of certain weight and size will tend to accumulate

where other objects and size have accumulated.

Some folks like to search in lines from up on the beach and back toward the water line. I like doing this myself. That way, I am sure that I have found about all there is to find in my search down the beach.

Some folks like to search in long lines parallel to the beach. I do this sometimes and get

decent results.

Some folks draw squares in the sand and search each individual square to be sure that

They have recovered all that they can recover from the part of the beach that they are

searching.

Now, go out into the sunshine and find your fair share of what there is to find. And I

sincerely hope that you have great luck and wonderful adventures. Good luck, and God bless.

www.ingramcontent.com/pod-product-compliance
Lightning Source LLC
Chambersburg PA
CBHW081325250726
48662CB00008B/2763